CONTENTS

Bacon & Potato Frittata

3 tablespoons butter or margarine
2 cups frozen O'Brien hash brown potatoes
   with onions and peppers
5 eggs
½ cup bacon, crisp-cooked and crumbled
¼ cup half-and-half or milk
⅛ teaspoon salt
⅛ teaspoon black pepper

1. Preheat broiler.

2. Melt butter in large ovenproof skillet over medium-high heat. Swirl butter up side of pan to prevent eggs from sticking. Add potatoes; cook 4 minutes, stirring occasionally.

3. Beat eggs in medium bowl. Add bacon, half-and-half, salt and pepper; mix well. Pour egg mixture into skillet; reduce heat to medium. Cover and cook 6 minutes or until eggs are set at edges (top will still be wet).

4. Transfer skillet to broiler. Broil 4 inches from heat 1 to 2 minutes or until golden brown and center is set. Cut into wedges.

Makes 4 to 6 servings

BLT Cukes

½ cup finely chopped lettuce
½ cup finely chopped baby spinach
3 slices bacon, crisp-cooked and crumbled
¼ cup finely diced tomato
1 tablespoon plus 1½ teaspoons mayonnaise
¼ teaspoon black pepper
⅛ teaspoon salt
1 large cucumber

1. Combine lettuce, spinach, bacon, tomato, mayonnaise, pepper and salt in medium bowl; mix well.

2. Peel cucumber; trim off ends and cut in half lengthwise. Use spoon to scoop out seeds; discard seeds.

3. Divide bacon mixture between cucumber halves, mounding in center. Cut into 2-inch pieces.

Makes 8 to 10 pieces

Bacon-Cheddar Muffins

2 cups all-purpose flour
¾ cup sugar
2 teaspoons baking powder
½ teaspoon baking soda
½ teaspoon salt
¾ cup plus 2 tablespoons milk
⅓ cup butter, melted and cooled
1 egg
1 cup (4 ounces) shredded Cheddar cheese
6 slices bacon, crisp-cooked and crumbled

1. Preheat oven to 350°F. Grease 12 standard (2½-inch) muffin cups.

2. Combine flour, sugar, baking powder, baking soda and salt in medium bowl. Combine milk, butter and egg in small bowl; mix well. Add milk mixture to flour mixture; stir just until blended. Gently stir in cheese and bacon. Spoon batter into prepared muffin cups, filling three-fourths full.

3. Bake 15 to 20 minutes or until toothpick inserted into centers comes out clean. Cool in pan 2 minutes; remove to wire rack. Serve warm or at room temperature. *Makes 12 muffins*

BACON BITS

When making muffins, don't grease any cups that won't be filled since the fat will burn and make your pan hard to clean. Instead, add two or three tablespoons of water to any empty cups to keep the pan from heating unevenly and/or warping in the oven.

Caramelized Bacon

12 slices (12 ounces) applewood-smoked bacon
½ cup packed light brown sugar
2 tablespoons water
¼ to ½ teaspoon ground red pepper

1. Preheat oven to 375°F. Line 15×10-inch jelly-roll pan with heavy-duty foil. Spray wire rack with nonstick cooking spray; place in prepared pan.

2. Cut bacon in half crosswise; arrange in single layer on prepared rack. Combine sugar, water and ground red pepper in small bowl; mix well. Brush generously over surface of bacon.

3. Bake 20 to 25 minutes or until bacon is dark brown. Immediately remove to serving platter; cool completely.   *Makes 6 servings*

Bacon Bits: Bacon can be prepared up to three days ahead and stored in the refrigerator between sheets of waxed paper in a large resealable food storage bag. Let stand at room temperature 30 minutes before serving.

Buckwheat Browns

1 cup cooked soba noodles, drained and chopped well
⅓ cup bacon, crisp-cooked and crumbled
⅓ cup minced fresh parsley
¼ cup minced red bell pepper
1 teaspoon minced garlic
1 egg white, beaten until foamy
½ teaspoon black pepper
Nonstick cooking spray

1. Mix noodles with bacon, parsley, bell pepper, garlic, egg white and black pepper in medium bowl; stir well. (Egg white should be partially absorbed.)

2. Spray large skillet with cooking spray; heat over medium-high heat. Use ¼ cup measure to scoop noodle mixture onto skillet. Cook 3 to 4 minutes. Spray each noodle cluster with cooking spray; turn and cook 3 to 4 minutes or until noodles are browned at edges. Serve warm.
Makes 6 servings

Bacon and Egg Cups

12 slices bacon, crisp-cooked and cut crosswise into thirds
6 eggs
½ cup diced bell pepper
½ cup (2 ounces) shredded pepper jack cheese
½ cup half-and-half
¼ teaspoon salt
¼ teaspoon black pepper

1. Preheat oven to 350°F. Lightly spray 12 standard (2½-inch) muffin cups with nonstick cooking spray.

2. Place 3 bacon slices in each prepared muffin cup, overlapping in bottom. Beat eggs, bell pepper, cheese, half-and-half, salt and black pepper in medium bowl until well blended. Fill each muffin cup with ¼ cup egg mixture.

3. Bake 20 to 25 minutes or until eggs are set in center. Run knife around edge of each cup to remove from pan.   *Makes 12 servings*

Bacon Bits: To save time, look for mixed diced bell peppers in the produce section of the grocery store.

Bacon and Cheese Brunch Potatoes

3 medium russet potatoes, cut into 1-inch pieces
1 cup chopped onion
½ teaspoon seasoned salt
4 slices bacon, crisp-cooked and crumbled
1 cup (4 ounces) shredded sharp Cheddar cheese
1 tablespoon chicken broth or water

SLOW COOKER DIRECTIONS

1. Coat slow cooker with nonstick cooking spray. Layer half of potatoes, onion, seasoned salt, bacon and cheese in slow cooker. Repeat layers, ending with cheese. Pour broth over top.

2. Cover; cook on LOW 6 hours or on HIGH 3½ hours. Stir gently to mix before serving.   *Makes 6 servings*

Simmered Split Pea Soup

3 cans (about 14 ounces each) chicken broth
1 package (16 ounces) dried split peas
8 slices bacon, crisp-cooked, crumbled and divided
1 onion, diced
2 carrots, diced
1 teaspoon black pepper
½ teaspoon dried thyme
1 bay leaf

SLOW COOKER DIRECTIONS

1. Combine broth, peas, half of bacon, onion, carrots, pepper, thyme and bay leaf in slow cooker. Cover; cook on LOW 6 to 8 hours.

2. Remove and discard bay leaf. Garnish with remaining half of bacon.

Makes 6 servings

Winter's Best Bean Soup

6 ounces bacon, crisp-cooked and diced
10 cups chicken broth
3 cans (about 15 ounces each) Great Northern beans,
   rinsed and drained
1 can (about 14 ounces) diced tomatoes
1 large onion, chopped
1 package (about 10 ounces) frozen diced carrots
2 teaspoons minced garlic
1 sprig fresh rosemary *or* 1 teaspoon dried rosemary
1 teaspoon black pepper

SLOW COOKER DIRECTIONS

1. Layer bacon, broth, beans, tomatoes, onion, carrots, garlic, rosemary and pepper in slow cooker.

2. Cover; cook on LOW 8 hours. Remove rosemary sprig before serving.

Makes 8 to 10 servings

Bacon-Wrapped Fingerling Potatoes with Thyme

1 pound fingerling potatoes
2 tablespoons olive oil
1 tablespoon minced fresh thyme, plus additional for garnish
½ teaspoon black pepper
¼ teaspoon paprika
½ pound bacon slices, cut in half lengthwise
¼ cup chicken broth

SLOW COOKER DIRECTIONS

1. Toss potatoes with oil, 1 tablespoon thyme, pepper and paprika in large bowl. Wrap half slice bacon tightly around each potato.

2. Heat large skillet over medium heat; add potatoes. Reduce heat to medium-low. Cook 7 minutes or until lightly browned and bacon has tightened around potatoes.

3. Place potatoes in 4½-quart slow cooker. Add broth. Cover; cook on HIGH 3 hours. Garnish with additional thyme.   *Makes 4 to 6 servings*

BACON BITS

This appetizer can be made even more eye-catching with rare varieties of potatoes. Many interesting varieties can be found at farmers' markets. Purple potatoes, about the size of fingerling potatoes, can add more color to this dish.

BLT Biscuits

2 cups all-purpose flour
2 teaspoons sugar
2 teaspoons baking powder
1 teaspoon black pepper
½ teaspoon baking soda
½ teaspoon salt
⅓ cup cold butter, cut into small pieces
1 cup (4 ounces) shredded Cheddar cheese
¾ cup buttermilk
½ cup mayonnaise
1 small head romaine lettuce, torn into small pieces
4 plum tomatoes, cut into ¼-inch slices
1 package (16 ounces) bacon slices, crisp-cooked and
　　cut crosswise into 3 pieces

1. Preheat oven to 425°F. Line baking sheets with parchment paper.

2. Combine flour, sugar, baking powder, pepper, baking soda and salt in large bowl. Cut in butter with pastry blender or two knives until mixture resembles coarse crumbs. Stir in cheese and buttermilk just until mixture forms dough.

3. Turn dough out onto lightly floured surface; knead gently several times. Pat into 8×6-inch rectangle (about ¾ inch thick). Cut dough into 24 squares with sharp knife; place on prepared baking sheets. Bake 10 to 12 minutes or until golden brown. Cool slightly on wire rack.

4. Split biscuits; spread each half lightly with mayonnaise. Layer each biscuit with lettuce, tomato and bacon. *Makes 24 mini sandwiches*

Turkey Club Biscuits: Prepare BLT Biscuits as directed above, adding deli sliced turkey and avocado slices.

Bacon-Wrapped Apricots

14 slices bacon, cut in half crosswise
¼ cup packed brown sugar
½ teaspoon black pepper
28 Mediterranean dried apricots (one 7-ounce package)
14 water chestnuts, drained and cut in half crosswise

1. Preheat oven to 425°F. Line shallow baking pan or baking sheet with parchment paper.

2. Sprinkle bacon with brown sugar and pepper, pressing to adhere. Fold apricot around water chestnut half. Wrap with half slice bacon; secure with toothpick.

3. Arrange apricots in prepared pan, spacing at least 1 inch apart. Bake 20 minutes or until bacon is cooked through, turning once.

Makes 14 servings

Spicy Deviled Eggs

6 eggs
3 tablespoons whipping cream
1 green onion, finely chopped
1 tablespoon white wine vinegar
2 teaspoons Dijon mustard
½ teaspoon curry powder
½ teaspoon hot pepper sauce
3 tablespoons bacon, crisp-cooked and crumbled

1. Place eggs in small saucepan; cover with water. Bring to a boil over high heat. Cover and remove from heat; let stand 15 minutes. Drain and rinse under cold water. Peel eggs; cool completely.

2. Slice eggs in half lengthwise. Remove yolks to small bowl; set whites aside. Mash yolks with fork. Stir in cream, green onion, vinegar, mustard, curry powder and hot pepper sauce until blended.

3. Spoon egg yolk mixture into centers of egg whites. Arrange eggs on serving plate. Sprinkle bacon over eggs.

Makes 12 deviled eggs

Western Barbecue Burgers with Beer Barbecue Sauce

1½ **pounds ground beef**
1 **cup smokehouse-style barbecue sauce**
¼ **cup brown ale**
½ **teaspoon salt**
¼ **teaspoon black pepper**
1 **red onion, cut into ½-inch-thick slices**
4 **hamburger buns**
8 **slices thick-sliced bacon, crisp-cooked**
    Lettuce leaves and sliced tomatoes

1. Prepare grill for direct cooking. Shape beef into 4 patties about ¾ inch thick.

2. Combine barbecue sauce, ale, salt and pepper in small saucepan. Bring to a boil; boil 1 minute. Remove from heat; set aside.

3. Grill patties over medium-high heat, covered, 8 to 10 minutes (or uncovered, 13 to 15 minutes) until cooked through (160°F) or to desired doneness, turning occasionally. Grill onion 4 minutes or until softened and slightly charred, turning occasionally.

4. Place patties on bottom halves of buns; top with onion, bacon and barbecue sauce mixture. Place lettuce and tomatoes on top halves of buns. *Makes 4 servings*

Bacon Roasted Brussels Sprouts

1 **pound Brussels sprouts**
3 **slices bacon, cut into ½-inch pieces**
2 **teaspoons packed brown sugar**
    Salt and black pepper

1. Preheat oven to 400°F. Trim ends from Brussels sprouts; cut in half lengthwise.

2. Combine Brussels sprouts, bacon and brown sugar in glass baking dish.

3. Bake 25 to 30 minutes or until golden brown, stirring once. Season with salt and pepper. *Makes 4 servings*

Western Barbecue Burgers with Beer Barbecue Sauce

Bacon & Tomato Melts

4 slices bacon, crisp-cooked
4 slices (1 ounce each) Cheddar cheese
1 medium tomato, sliced
4 slices whole wheat bread
2 tablespoons butter, melted

1. Layer 2 slices bacon, 2 slices cheese and tomato on each of 2 bread slices; top with remaining bread slices. Brush sandwiches with butter.

2. Heat large skillet over medium heat. Add sandwiches; press lightly with spatula. Cook 4 to 5 minutes per side or until cheese melts and sandwiches are golden brown. *Makes 2 sandwiches*

Chicken, Bacon and Vegetable Sandwiches

½ cup mayonnaise
¼ teaspoon garlic powder
½ teaspoon black pepper, divided
4 boneless skinless chicken breasts (about 1¼ pounds)
1 green bell pepper, cut into quarters
1 medium zucchini, cut lengthwise into 4 slices
3 tablespoons olive oil
2 cloves garlic, minced
1½ teaspoons dried basil
½ teaspoon salt
4 ciabatta or focaccia rolls, halved
2 Italian plum tomatoes, sliced
4 slices Provolone cheese
8 slices bacon, crisp-cooked

1. Preheat broiler. Combine mayonnaise, garlic powder and ¼ teaspoon black pepper in small bowl; set aside. Combine chicken, bell pepper, zucchini, oil, garlic, basil, salt and remaining ¼ teaspoon black pepper in large resealable food storage bag. Seal bag; knead to combine.

2. Broil chicken, bell pepper and zucchini 4 inches from heat 6 to 8 minutes on each side or until chicken is no longer pink in center. Layer bottom halves of rolls with mayonnaise mixture, zucchini, tomatoes, bell pepper, chicken, cheese, bacon and top halves of rolls.

Makes 4 sandwiches

Bacon & Tomato Melt

Bacon and Blue Cheese Stuffed Burgers

4 slices applewood-smoked bacon or regular bacon
1 small red onion, finely chopped
2 tablespoons crumbled blue cheese
1 tablespoon butter, softened
1½ pounds ground beef
   Salt and black pepper
4 onion or plain hamburger rolls
   Lettuce leaves

1. Cook bacon in large skillet over medium-high heat until chewy but not crisp. Drain on paper towels. Chop into small pieces. Add onion to drippings in skillet; cook until soft. Cool.

2. Combine bacon, onion, blue cheese and butter in small bowl; mix well. Prepare grill for direct cooking.

3. Shape beef into 8 thin patties about 4 inches wide. Season patties with salt and pepper. Place 2 tablespoons bacon mixture in center of 1 patty; cover with another patty. Pinch edges together to seal. Shape burger until round and slightly flattened. Repeat with remaining patties and cheese mixture.

4. Grill patties over medium-high heat, covered, 8 to 10 minutes (or uncovered, 13 to 15 minutes) until cooked through (160°F) or to desired doneness, turning occasionally. Serve burgers on rolls with lettuce.

Makes 4 servings

 **BACON BITS**

If you want juicy, flavorful burgers, do not flatten patties. Pressing down on the patties with a spatula not only squeezes out tasty juices, but in this recipe it might also cause the stuffing to pop out.

Farm-Raised Catfish with Bacon and Horseradish

6 (4- to 5-ounce) farm-raised catfish fillets
2 tablespoons butter
¼ cup chopped onion
1 (8-ounce) package cream cheese, softened
¼ cup dry white wine
2 tablespoons prepared horseradish
1 tablespoon Dijon mustard
½ teaspoon salt
⅛ teaspoon black pepper
4 slices bacon, crisp-cooked and crumbled
Lettuce leaves (optional)

1. Preheat oven to 350°F. Grease large baking dish. Arrange fillets in single layer in prepared dish.

2. Melt butter in small skillet over medium-high heat. Add onion; cook and stir until softened. Combine cream cheese, wine, horseradish, mustard, salt and pepper in small bowl; stir in onion. Pour over fish and top with crumbled bacon.

3. Bake 30 minutes or until fish begins to flake when tested with fork. Serve on lettuce leaves. *Makes 6 servings*

Bacon-Wrapped BBQ Chicken

8 chicken tenders (about 1 pound)
8 slices bacon
½ cup barbecue sauce

1. Preheat broiler. Line broiler pan with foil.

2. Wrap each chicken tender with slice of bacon in spiral pattern; place on prepared pan.

3. Broil chicken 4 minutes. Turn and broil 2 minutes. Brush with ¼ cup barbecue sauce; broil 2 minutes. Turn and brush with remaining ¼ cup barbecue sauce; broil 2 minutes or until chicken is no longer pink in center. *Makes 4 servings*

Farm-Raised Catfish with Bacon and Horseradish

Brisket with Bacon, Blue Cheese and Onions

2 large sweet onions,* sliced into ½-inch rounds
6 slices bacon, divided
1 flat-cut boneless beef brisket (about 3½ pounds)
   Salt and black pepper
2 cans (about 14 ounces each) beef broth
1 teaspoon cracked black peppercorns
3 ounces crumbled blue cheese

*Maui, Vidalia or Walla Walla onions are preferred.

SLOW COOKER DIRECTIONS

1. Coat 5- to 6-quart slow cooker with nonstick cooking spray. Line bottom with onion slices.

2. Heat large skillet over medium-high heat. Add bacon and cook until chewy but not crisp. Drain on paper towels. Chop bacon.

3. Season brisket with salt and pepper. Sear brisket in bacon drippings on all sides. Remove to slow cooker.

4. Pour broth in slow cooker. Sprinkle with peppercorns and half of bacon. Cover; cook on HIGH 5 to 7 hours.

5. Remove brisket to cutting board; cover with foil. Let stand 10 minutes. Slice against the grain into ¾-inch slices.

6. To serve, arrange brisket slices on plates; top with onions, blue cheese and remaining bacon. Season cooking liquid with salt and pepper; serve with brisket.   *Makes 6 to 8 servings*

BLT Chicken Salad for Two

2 boneless skinless chicken breasts
¼ cup mayonnaise or salad dressing
½ teaspoon black pepper
4 large lettuce leaves
1 large tomato, seeded and diced
3 slices bacon, crisp-cooked and crumbled
1 hard-cooked egg, sliced
   Prepared salad dressing

1. Prepare grill for direct cooking.

2. Brush chicken with mayonnaise; sprinkle with pepper. Grill over medium heat 5 to 7 minutes per side or until no longer pink in center. Cool slightly; cut into thin strips.

3. Arrange lettuce on serving plates. Top with chicken, tomato, bacon and egg. Serve with salad dressing.   *Makes 2 servings*

Nine-Layer Salad

6 cups baby spinach, packed
1½ cups grape tomatoes
2 cups pattypan squash, halved crosswise
1 cup peas, blanched
4 ounces baby corn, halved lengthwise
2 cups baby carrots, blanched and halved lengthwise
1 cup peppercorn-ranch salad dressing
1 cup (4 ounces) shredded Cheddar cheese
4 slices bacon, crisp-cooked and crumbled

1. Layer spinach, tomatoes, squash, peas, corn and carrots in 4-quart glass bowl. Pour dressing over salad; spread evenly. Top with cheese. Cover and refrigerate 4 hours.

2. Sprinkle with bacon before serving.   *Makes 7 servings*